Ways to Pray

David Thomson

PATERNOSTER PRESS

MILTON KEYNES • COLORADO SPRINGS • HYDERABAD

CONTENTS

'When you pray, do not be like the hypocrites, for they love to pray standing in the synagogues and on the street corners to be seen by men. I tell you the truth, they have received their reward in full. But when you pray, go into your room, close the door and pray to your Father, who is unseen. Then your Father, who sees what is done in secret, will reward you. And when you pray, do not keep on babbling like pagans, for they think they will be heard because of their many words. Do not be like them, for your Father knows what you need before you ask him. This, then, is how you should pray: "Our Father in heaven, hallowed be your name, your kingdom come, your will be done on earth as it is in heaven. Give us today our daily bread. Forgive us our debts, as we also have forgiven our debtors. And lead us not into temptation, but deliver us from the evil one." For if you forgive men when they sin against you, your heavenly Father will also forgive you. But if you do not forgive men their sins, your Father will not forgive your sins. Ask and it will be given to you; seek and you will find; knock and the door will be opened to you. For everyone who asks receives; he who seeks finds; and to him who knocks, the door will be opened. Which of you, if his son asks for bread, will give him a stone? Or if he asks for a fish, will give him a snake? If you, then, though you are evil, know how to give good gifts to your children, how much more will your Father in heaven give good gifts to those who ask him! So in everything, do to others what you would have them do to you, for this sums up the Law and the Prophets.'

Matthew 6.5-15; 7.7-12

One day Jesus was praying in a certain place. When he finished, one of his disciples said to him, 'Lord, teach us to pray, just as John taught his disciples.' He said to them, 'When you pray, say: "Father, hallowed be your name, your kingdom come. Give us each day our daily bread. Forgive us our sins, for we also forgive everyone who sins against us. And lead us not into temptation." '

Then he said to them, 'Suppose one of you has a friend, and he goes to him at midnight and says, "Friend, lend me three loaves of bread, because a friend of mine on a journey has come to me, and I have nothing to set before him." Then the one inside answers, "Don't bother me. The door is already locked, and my children are with me in bed. I can't get up and give you anything." I tell you, though he will not get up and give him the bread because he is his friend, yet because of the man's boldness he will get up and give him as much as he needs.

'So I say to you: Ask and it will be given to you; seek and you will find; knock and the door will be opened to you. For everyone who asks receives; he who seeks finds; and to him who knocks, the door will be opened.

'Which of you fathers, if your son asks for a fish, will give him a snake instead? Or if he asks for an egg, will give him a scorpion? If you then, though you are evil, know how to give good gifts to your children, how much more will your Father in heaven give the Holy Spirit to those who ask him!'

Luke 11.1-13

Introduction

This is not the book of an expert! I find prayer difficult to get round to, and difficult to stay with, and if I talk about its problems it's because I know them first hand. But I have been convinced for over twenty-five years now that without prayer we're sunk as God's people. The Son invites us into this most remarkable relationship with the Father, and into it pours the gifts of the Spirit. It is the archetypal activity of the Christian, and the key to the Kingdom's coming. Great saints have given us the record of their lives lived this way with God – from Augustine and Anselm to Julian and John of the Cross, from Teresa of Avila and Thomas á Kempis to the Wesleys and Somerset Ward; and then we've only just begun. These scribblings are not in that league! They are basics for the early days when ideas are being explored, habits formed and routines set; or for those pause-for-thought moments later when we take stock of our story so far.

This is a practical sort of book – more of a 'course' or study-guide really. So before the pilgrimage comes the packing. What might you need in your knapsack before you get going? A working Bible is a pre-requisite – preferably one you don't mind writing all over as your prayer journey develops; it's a great place to record the insights and issues, words and worries that accompany us, leaving them with God but ready to be found again when we need them. Some sort of journal to write in seems to help most people too – the margins of your Bible are only so big, and anyway a more chronological account of your comings and goings with space to really pour out your heart is an asset. If there is a volume of set prayers or services that you like, and/or a book or scheme of Bible reading and study, put that in the pile too. And that's about it.

Each chapter is put together to provide the basis of an hour or two's reading and prayer. You'll find stories, quotations and nudges to action, together with:

- Something to help you get still
- An opportunity to reflect on the journey so far
- A visit to the 'Prayer Clinic', tackling one of the common problems we face (often picking up an issue the previous chapter may have raised)
- An exercise to build on that
- A teaching slot, taking its lead from a line of the Lord's Prayer
- A second exercise
- Something to round things off
- And a thought for the week or day ahead

A final chapter gives some ideas for the future, focussed on the theme of pilgrimage, and the book finishes with a selection of favourite prayers, and some suggestions for further reading.

You could read a chapter a week, during a period such as Lent or between Easter and Pentecost if you like a link with the Church Year; or you could look at a chapter a day and zoom through in a week, though you will only make the most of a journey at that speed, I think, if you are on retreat, or have a decent amount of time to live with the prayer between the sessions. Otherwise you'll probably end up knowing a few things about how prayer should be, but without much change in how your own prayer is. Slow is good!

You could also easily use the book together in a group, Lent or otherwise: in fact that's how it first began life, as a course for the congregations in the parishes of Cockermouth, Embleton and Wythop, where I was Team Rector at the time. Using the book together also brings the great benefit that we can help each other along the road. Although prayer is very personal, that does not mean that it is always meant to be private; and although we all pray in different ways, putting them together brings wholeness and strength.

I'd like to record my huge thanks to all my friends from those days: there is a lot of them in here. There is nearly nothing in the book, in fact, that is really original. So much praying has been practised, so many books and courses and talks and sermons written about it, that there is little room for me to be anything other than a snapper up of trifles, hopefully not wholly unconsidered, or a dwarf on the shoulders on giants, occasionally glimpsing the way ahead, but always in danger of over-estimating my own stature.

I haven't tried to give references for all the material I have drawn on and quotations I have cited, much of which is common circulation, but the more significant ones are given at the end of the book. If anything has slipped through without proper acknowledgement, please accept my apologies and let the publishers know so that we can put things right. But I would like to say a special word of thanks to the authors whose work I have cited at the end of the book to whom I owe a great deal; to the usual suspects who have helped the book into being, Jeremy Mudditt, Charlotte Hubback and Kath Williams at Authentic, and Chris Lawther at Teamwork; to Tricia for the typing; and above all to Jean who is with me all along the way, and is so often the one who keeps me safe and sane. All the really odd and silly bits are of course mine alone.

David Thomson, Summer 2007, Carlisle

1 Our Father in Heaven

Be Still

Keep quiet for a moment and light a candle in front of you. This candle can be lit during whenever you use the book, as a reminder that God is with us in our struggles to pray, and sends His Spirit to help us. After a few moments of quiet, say the Lord's Prayer.

Our Father in heaven,	Our Father, who art in heaven,
hallowed be your name,	hallowed be thy name;
your kingdom come,	thy kingdom come;
your will be done,	thy will be done;
on earth as in heaven.	on earth as it is in heaven.
Give us today our daily bread.	Give us this day our daily bread
Forgive us our sins	and forgive us our trespasses,
as we forgive those	as we forgive those
who sin against us.	who trespass against us.
Lead us not into temptation	And lead us not into temptation;
but deliver us from evil.	but deliver us from evil.
For the kingdom, the power,	For thine is the kingdom,
and the glory are yours,	the power and the glory,
now and for ever. Amen.	for ever and ever. Amen.

The Journey so far

Call to mind your feelings as you start this prayer journey, and perhaps begin a journal by noting them down. You could add, in a big box, that useful motto: 'Pray as you can, not as you can't.' Also, if one comes to mind, jot down a prayer that has been special to you, or the first prayer you remember learning or using, besides the Lord's Prayer. Who taught or gave it to you?

Then just be quiet again for a little while – before your first visit to the Prayer Clinic.

Prayer Clinic: *Finding Time to Pray*

Welcome to the Clinic! Just by turning up (Woody Allen said it was 80% of life ...) you have already made a start in getting to grips with prayer, and getting started is the first subject I want to tackle. Nearly all of us find there is a difficult gap between how we would like to be in prayer – regular, committed, godly – and how we really end up as soon as the pressures of daily life take over again.

In Chapter 11 of his Gospel, St Luke records how the disciples came to Jesus and asked, 'Lord, teach us how to pray'. I wonder if they were in the same position as us. Jesus' reply was to teach them the Lord's Prayer, but first, according to St Matthew, he instructed them to go to their room and close the door. So often our problem is just that: finding a time and space to pray in, somewhere quiet and undisturbed. Jesus' teaching, though, suggests that we do have to find a way through this if our prayer is to take off.

So, how can we do it? One key to the answer is to remember that each of us must pray as we can, not as we can't. That means here that, because each of our personal circumstances is different, each of us will also have a different time, place and even posture that is right for us when we pray. And that may change over time. When our youngest daughter, Caitlin, was small, she used to come into bed with me in the early morning and I would make up stories for her. Then, when Jean had surfaced and taken over with the routine, I would stay propped up in bed and say morning prayer. Once Caitlin was older and we were getting up early for school, I'd wait until the coast was clear and sink into the armchair in my study, where I had a cross and candle on the shelf, a few helpful books, and a stereo set up with meditative music. Years later, I find I am living a stone's throw from a cathedral, and after some prayer for my family and the clergy and parishes in my care over a morning cuppa, I crawl out of bed and across for Matins in my cassock. (I think the tradition must have arisen to disguise the state of the cleric within it ...)

In her book *Learning the Language of Prayer*, Joyce Huggett tells us of three women she met whose prayer places were quite different. One, whose

Quote – unquote

The real problem of the Christian life comes where people do not usually look for it. It comes the very moment you wake up each morning. All your wishes and hopes for the day rush at you like wild animals. And the first job every morning consists in shoving them all back; in listening to that other voice, taking that other point of view, letting that other larger, stronger, quieter life come flowing in. ... We can do it only for a few moments at first. But from those moments the new sort of life will be spreading through our systems because now we are letting him work at the right part of us.

C S Lewis, 'Mere Christianity'

husband was not a Christian, had an agreement with him that, when she was sitting in the chair in the corner of the bedroom, she was not to be disturbed. Another, a Singaporean in a busy home, went early to the office and prayed there before her colleagues arrived. A third, whose unemployed husband could not stand her praying, prayed with her eyes shut during the TV commercials, which did not upset him as he thought she was sleeping!

But what about you? Forget big rules like having to start the day with a quiet time, or having to kneel, or be in a church to pray. What does experience tell you is a quiet time of the day for you? Is it sitting, kneeling, standing, squatting or walking – or even lying on the floor as I heard from one person recently – that is most comfortable for prayer for you? Also, which place has that special feel: the living room, bedroom, conservatory, garden, kitchen? Or perhaps the bath!

It really is best to begin in this practical way. Do find what is **right** for you – but do let it be what is right for **you**. In C S Lewis' famous *Screwtape Letters*, the senior devil writes to his younger colleague about his 'patients': 'at least they can be persuaded that the bodily position makes no difference to their prayers; for they constantly forget, what you and I must always remember, that they are animals and that whatever their bodies do affects their souls.' Lewis wrote too, in one of his *Letters to Malcolm* that, 'What pleases me most about a Greek Orthodox mass I once attended was that there seemed to be no prescribed behaviour for the congregation; some stood, some knelt, some sat, some walked; one crawled about the floor like a caterpillar. The beauty of it was that nobody took the slightest notice of what anyone else was doing.' If we are going to get praying, we will need to find our own time, our own place, our own posture; and it is quite all right to be different from the person next door.

> **Quote – unquote**
> In prayer it is better to have a heart without words than words without a heart.
> *Mahatma Gandhi*

Exercise

Can you remember times/places/postures that have been helpful for you in prayer before, or not helpful at all? Try one out for a moment or two and see if you were right. Or have things changed? Then have a stretch, – and a scribble in your journal.

Teaching talk

So, we want to start praying and, perhaps, we have taken the first step of setting aside a time and place for that purpose: an essential step, not only for practical reasons, but because it means we are willing to make room for God in our lives, even if it costs us something. What next?

Most of us grow up thinking of prayer as asking for things. That is important and we will come to it later, but in the Lord's Prayer 'give us this day our daily bread' is quite a long way down the list. We begin 'Our Father': and there is a good reason for doing so. The discovery that God is like a Father to us was one of the greatest insights that Jesus passed on to his disciples. The whole Lord's Prayer is set by St Luke in the context of Jesus' teaching about the Father and, if God is as personal, as loving, as special to us as that can be, then getting our relationship right with Him comes before asking for things.

Think of it for a moment in human terms. (Limited though they are, they give us good clues). God understands that, sometimes, we are in an emergency, and, whether He is a stranger or well-known to us, He does not turn us away in our need. Like any parent, He longs for us not just to come to Him when we need things, but to be with Him just because we are His family. The same is true of any marriage or friendship.

Quote - unquote

Our Father in heaven: That to me is crucial …. There are some people who have difficulty with the Our Father because they have had an abusive father, so the word 'Father' is hateful to them. And then, I would imagine, they have to spend a long time in prayer understanding the difference. … His is the kind of fatherhood that is beyond anybody's imagining.

Wendy Beckett, 'Living the Lord's Prayer'

Big Issue

For such a short prayer, the Our Father raises a lot of big issues that are very relevant to us and our society today. One here is **trust**: trust in God, the Good Father, and trust in one another as His family. We live in a culture of suspicion, and pay the price in regulation and law-suits. How can we break free?

So, prayer begins not with petitions but a relationship in which we can talk things over with God, enjoy His company without words, just know His presence. That means that starting to pray is paradoxically about stopping. We have to switch off to the other noises and concerns around us and give God our attention. In the words of Psalm 46, to 'Be still and know that I am God'.

Stopping, slowing down, relaxing: these are things that most of us find very hard: which is, of course, another reason why prayer can be so frustrating. It is worth tackling this head on because, again, if we try to bypass it we will find progress very difficult. Prayer will always seem one-sided, arrows of hope-against-hope shot off into the dark.

Psalm 46

1 God is our refuge and strength,
an ever-present help in trouble.
2 Therefore we will not fear, though the earth give way
and the mountains fall into the heart of the sea,
3 though its waters roar and foam
and the mountains quake with their surging. *Selah*
4 There is a river whose streams make glad the city of God,
the holy place where the Most High dwells.
5 God is within her, she will not fall;
God will help her at break of day.
6 Nations are in uproar, kingdoms fall;
he lifts his voice, the earth melts.
7 The LORD Almighty is with us;
the God of Jacob is our fortress. *Selah*
8 Come and see the works of the LORD,
the desolations he has brought on the earth.
9 He makes wars cease to the ends of the earth;
he breaks the bow and shatters the spear,
he burns the shields with fire.
10 'Be still, and know that I am God;
I will be exalted among the nations,
I will be exalted in the earth.'
11 The LORD Almighty is with us;
the God of Jacob is our fortress. *Selah*

I would like to describe one way of entering into the stillness of our relationship with the Father in heaven. In this way, we begin with the things we were talking about earlier: time, place and posture, settling down as best we can. I will assume, for the moment, that you have chosen to sit, as that is probably what you are doing now. As I describe the steps that follow, you could practise them quietly, if you want to.

First, we need to take note of our body. We usually find that there are aches and pains and, in particular, quite a lot of muscular tension. Some of that is just working quietly away to keep us from toppling over. But some is locked around a physical or mental hurt or worry and, if we can, we need to relax it. A good way is to become aware of each muscle group in turn, tense it and loosen it a couple of times, then move on to the next. Try imaging yourself wearing an outsize stripy dress or rugger shirt which reaches right down to your toes. Then give the relaxation treatment to each stripe in turn: toes first, then calves and so on, up to the top. The last bit is to give your face a really good grimace or two: it is surprising how much tension can be locked up there too

Then, hopefully a little more relaxed, it is best to sit back into the chair, reasonably straight-backed, hands on knees, feet on floor, and let your breathing settle into a comfortable rhythm. It can help to repeat a short phrase or sentence – a prayer or Bible verse is best, silently in time with your breathing. 'Be still and know that I am God'; 'Lord Jesus Christ, Son of the Living God, have mercy on me, a sinner' (The 'Jesus Prayer'); 'Fill me Lord and I shall be filled'. Choose words which are natural for you and which express a real need or feeling you have before God. In the Eastern Church, the saints would keep a prayer like this on their breath for a lifetime. I suggest that three or four minutes might be a reasonable initial target for us!

Next, we let our attention focus on some object that speaks to us of the presence of God: a natural object; a candle; a cross; an icon; an arrangement of flowers. Then, attentive to that focus, we listen for God. Do not struggle too much at first, though, to hear what He is saying. Just try to nestle in His love and accept whatever feelings of peace, passion or even sleep arise. Jesus said in His teaching on prayer that, if we can trust our earthly fathers to give us good things, how much more can we trust God. Give Him a try.

Exercise

Attempt the method of prayer just described. If you can, allow the silence to be held for a good ten minutes. Where there is deep-rooted pain

Story Box: One frail bark

The word in Psalm 46 to 'Be still' came precisely in the context of a time of trouble. And life brings plenty of troubles, so we really need to face up to the issue straight away. Trusting is easy when everything is going fine. Some people seem to believe that as long as we pray properly in faith horrible things won't happen. I am not one of them. Too many awful things happen to good and bad people alike. Sometimes, the worst does happen; and then I am driven back to a deeper sense of trust in a Father God whose goodness and love, like that of an earthly parent at its best, is with us and for us - whatever. 'Father' can trip off the tongue easily enough. I was brought up short in my use of it when I visited Ashbourne Church in Derbyshire and saw this most poignant memorial of parental love when I was in quite a state myself after a mishap with my car.

> To Penelope, Only child of Sir Brooke and Dame Svanna
>
> BOOTHBY.
>
> Born April XI. MDCCLXXXV Died March XIII. MDCCXCI
>
> She was in form and intellect most exqvisite
>
> The vnfortvnate parents ventvred their all
>
> On this frail bark and the wreck was total

Penelope's parents must have been devastated. Even in my minor catastrophe I found myself curling up, closing my eyes, and praying that I'd just wake up in bed at home and find it had all been a dream. How much more must they have longed for that. Nestle up – but nestle into God, not oblivion. Human resources can quickly run out. God's don't. His promise is one of redemption, not rewind: He can make new facts out of old ones. And sometimes, in extremis, we simply have to keep digging out the whole well of despair until we strike the living water at its very bottom. After all, He has ventured His all on our frail barks, and the shipwreck that was ours has been bottomed by His.

or tiredness, it will often surface before God's presence and peace is experienced. This is quite normal and the beginning of healing, like a temporary plaster being peeled back from a wound so that it can be dressed properly.

Drawing it together

Say a simple prayer – perhaps one of the favourites from earlier on – and the grace. Then blow out the candle until next time.

Thought for the week

Stay with your chosen time and place of prayer for a week, try out various ways of being still, and keep a note in your journal of how it goes.

ACTION STATIONS

Prayer that becomes detached from our active lives can become a dangerous distraction for all except the true contemplatives: and they make the connection too though in a different way. So this week – what are your actual relationships with the people around you like?

'Pray as though everything depended on God. Work as though everything depended on you.' *St Augustine*

---

2 Hallowed be Your Name

Be Still

Settle down, light your candle, and hallow your special place with a 'Circling Prayer' or Caim, like this old one from the Celtic tradition:

Circle us Lord,
Keep love within, keep hatred out.
Keep joy within, keep fear out.
Keep peace within, keep worry out.
Keep light within, keep darkness out.
May you stand in the circle with us, today and always.

The Journey so far

Look back at your journal. What did you find in the stillness with God? Presence? Absence? A word? Silence? Peace? Apprehension? Distractions? Concerns? Would it be a good idea to share these with someone?

Prayer Clinic: *Distractions*

If you are anything like me, you will find yourself experiencing a whole range of feelings and thoughts as you begin to take the risk of opening yourself to God's presence. For some, of course, it can be a wonderful time of refreshing peace: that is God's ultimate goal for us all. But for many, it can first be painful and, if so, do be reassured that you are not the black sheep of God's family. We all carry hurts and where better for them to surface than in the Father's arms. For some, it can be lonely, as if no-one is there, and I want to come back to that later. Again, it is something nearly everyone has to go through. For some, it can be sheer frustration, as all our attempts to be quiet are disturbed by distractions. And that is the problem, distraction, on which I want to focus now.

Distraction is a common problem because it comes in so many ways. First, we can face purely physical distractions: mundane things like the plumbing, the milkman, the telephone and the traffic. Or our body gets cramp or we need the loo. By and large, these things are not things we can control – so don't try. Accept them as God's gift and try to make your response to them an acted prayer. If you find your chosen place or time of prayer is being repeatedly interrupted, look for another.

Secondly, after physical distractions come mental ones. These are not evil or sinful: just our mind still running on in its usual overdrive. We suddenly remember that we should have phoned someone; or start thinking about some problem and get stuck on it. These distractions arise inside us, and if we try to ignore them they will tend – like attention-seeking children – to just shout louder. It is best, instead, to accept them and vent them by writing them down, a note to yourself to deal with them later, and then going back to the main task in hand. Occasionally you may, however, have the feeling that this 'distraction' is in fact being surfaced in your mind by God so that you can pray about it. If so, you will be able to pray with extra confidence and boldness, knowing that this is what God wants, say 'Amen' with conviction, and then return to your main pattern of prayer.

> **Quote – unquote**
>
> The time of business does not with me differ from the time of PRAYER, and in the noise and clatter of my kitchen, while several persons are at the same time calling for different things, I possess God as if I were upon my knees at the blessed sacrament.
>
> *Brother Lawrence*

> **Quote – unquote**
>
> The Lord's Prayer, for a succession of solemn thoughts, for fixing the attention upon a few great points, for suitableness to every condition, for sufficiency, for conciseness without obscurity, for the weight and real importance of its petition, is without an equal or a rival.
>
> *William Paley*

Lastly, there is spiritual distraction. The forces of evil, however you want to describe them, do not sit comfortably with our desire to pray, and so we are prey to their temptations, be they dead ends, sidetracks, sins or delusions. But don't be alarmed! Prayer is a bit like medicine: if it has come from a proper source, it will of course be clear about the problems to watch out for. It's good to read the label – but not so good to become obsessed by it. Our job is to take and trust the good medicine itself and seek help if we do encounter problems or get into a pickle, or find it hard to avoid trying out other 'treatments' that don't go well with it. So, be sensible: if the silence seems to draw you towards something that is sinful, or brings a voice that does not say what Jesus would say, just say 'no' to it in Jesus' name, give yourself a shake, and start again. If it keeps bothering you, have a word with a wise minister and you'll soon have it sorted.

Above all, in facing distraction of any sort, try to take a deep breath, say 'don't panic!', and learn to take it in your stride.

Exercise

This form of meditation is loosely based on one drawn up by St Ignatius in his famous *Spiritual Exercises* and is a way of making a virtue of a generally distracting prayer environment. Go through the getting still process that you learnt last week. When all is still, pray briefly aloud that God will fill the quiet with His presence and love, and fill your heart with the desire to love Him in return. Then, listen for the quietest, furthest away sounds you can and, as you hear each one, imagine God's love for whatever is happening there and to try and share in that feeling of love yourself. Then, progressively, let your attention focus on nearer and louder sounds. At some point, you will reach yourself. The meditation ends with remembering how much God loves us and allowing ourselves to respond to that love by pouring out a thankful love towards God Himself. Allow about 10 minutes for the meditation time.

Quote – unquote

Do not forget prayer. Every time you pray, if your prayer is sincere, there will be new feeling and new meaning in it, which will give you fresh courage.

Fyodor Dostoevsky

Teaching talk

I said earlier that we would come back to feelings of emptiness and loneliness in prayer. These can be symptoms of a prayer life which is moving on beyond its first steps, in which case, you will perhaps understand me if I offer both my congratulations and my condolences. We have to accept that prayer is always a struggle and going further on the journey means going further with the struggle. We will touch on this again in the next clinic but, if you feel that your prayer life is being taken into this wilderness or dark night, as it is sometimes called, you really should

Quote – unquote

Pray inwardly, even if you do not enjoy it. It does good, though you feel nothing, see nothing, yes, even though you think you are doing nothing. For when you are dry, empty, sick or weak, at such time is your prayer most pleasing, though you find little enough to enjoy in it. This is true of all believing prayer.

Julian of Norwich

consider setting up an ongoing relationship with another experienced person of prayer, a spiritual director, soul-friend or whatever: the words don't matter. If this is a new thought, or you are not sure how to take the first step, have a word with your minister and they will try to help.

In another, more basic way, though, emptiness and dryness in our prayer life can simply be a sign that it needs to be filled, to be hallowed by God's presence. We have succeeded in setting aside the props that the world offers us and now we need to know, and are ready to receive, God's presence. This is an important feature of Christian prayer. Some spiritual traditions just focus on self-emptying. As Christians, we deny ourselves only to take up the Cross and we make space in our hearts only that God can fill it.

God's presence and filling comes to us in three important ways. The best way is for us to learn to use and enjoy all three. But, as always, we are made differently and one way may come more naturally to us and be a good place to start.

First, God is the Creator, so the whole of creation speaks of His glory. So too do what J R R Tolkien called our works of sub-creation, the human creativity which we have as a gift from God and as part of His image in us, so that our lesser works of creation in music, painting, gardening, can speak of His presence as well as our skill. We can dwell on all these things, created and sub-created, and let them speak to us of God.

Secondly, God is Word, and the Bible, both as God's Word in itself and as the record of Jesus the Word Incarnate, clearly speaks to us in a way we can readily hear.

Thirdly, God is Spirit, and the Spirit too can speak to us in words of knowledge and wisdom, leading us into all truth and reminding us of Jesus'

Story Box: Living Water

A special friend invited us to join her in a meditation. After we became still, we pictured ourselves as having glass bodies – and very mucky insides! What to do? An angel kindly points out that our fingers and toes have stoppers at their ends: we remove them, one by one, and a lot of the gunge flows out – but some is stuck. Now what? Scarily, the angel points out that the top of our head is also detachable. Will we? Yes, he lifts it back, and through us pours from a pitcher water from the well of life. Wow! Flowing right through us it washes us more brilliantly than Bold. If only we could stay here for ever. But – back go the little stoppers, one by one, and slowly we feel ourselves fill from the bottom up with the living water, until finally we are put back together and the angel departs.

own words once more. So, we can invite the Spirit to do these things and be careful to note down what we hear and give it our respectful attention.

For now, though, I would like to focus on how the Bible can fill our prayer life with God's presence. The usual word for this process is meditation. The Church fathers compared it to chewing the cud! At its simplest, meditation is chewing over the Bible, reading it slowly, listening for God's word to us through it. This was the staple diet of many a monk, slowly copying the Scriptures by hand and learning to read, mark, learn and inwardly digest each verse as it was written. You might like to try producing your own slowly written illuminated chapter of the Bible as a way of entering into this experience.

Big Issue

'God's presence': is anything sacred today? When everything is 'affirmed', maybe nothing is really special; when everything is 'included' maybe nothing is ultimately other; when our choice is made a god, what happens to the God who chooses us? And to us?

Another way, developed by St Ignatius and now widespread through the writings of Joyce Huggett, is to use our imagination to let the Bible come to life for us. A Bible story is read to us or by us, perhaps twice, rather slowly. Then, asking the Holy Spirit to guide us, we begin to recollect it in our minds and, as we do so, we invite each of our five senses to come into operation, seeking to see, smell, hear, feel, taste the scene before us. Perhaps we take the part of one of the characters, or place ourselves in the crowd or as a bystander. As we do so, we are attentive to what the situation and, in

Using Art

In front of the south wall of the transept in Ely Cathedral is a sculpture by David Wynne of the moving encounter between Jesus and Mary Magdalene on the first Easter Day. The thinness of the figures is designed to command attention. The fragile legs are planted firmly, but the arms become a dance, nearly but not quite intertwining. There is a world of love, drawn together but distanced, in their expressions. Perhaps you will find that works of art help you get started in entering into the stories of Jesus – or perhaps you will prefer to start from scratch.

particular, what Jesus is saying to us. Many people have experienced such a word from our Lord in a remarkably vivid and helpful way.

Be warned: when God speaks to us in meditative prayer, He is working in the realm of the conscious mind and challenges our will, asks us to make choices, to adopt His strategy or point of view. Remember that, after hallowing God's name in the Lord's Prayer, we move straight on to pray that His kingdom will come and His will be done: beginning with us. That will be the theme of our study next week.

Exercise

Move into stillness as before, and pray for the guidance of God's Spirit. Then read Matthew 20.17-28.

> Now as Jesus was going up to Jerusalem, he took the twelve disciples aside and said to them, 'We are going up to Jerusalem, and the Son of Man will be betrayed to the chief priests and the teachers of the law. They will condemn him to death and will turn him over to the Gentiles to be mocked and flogged and crucified. On the third day he will be raised to life!'
>
> Then the mother of Zebedee's sons came to Jesus with her sons and, kneeling down, asked a favour of him. 'What is it you want?' he asked. She said, 'Grant that one of these two sons of mine may sit at your right and the other at your left in your kingdom.'
>
> 'You don't know what you are asking,' Jesus said to them. 'Can you drink the cup I am going to drink?' 'We can,' they answered. Jesus said to them, 'You will indeed drink from my cup, but to sit at my right or left is not for me to grant. These places belong to those for whom they have been prepared by my Father.'
>
> When the ten heard about this, they were indignant with the two brothers. Jesus called them together and said, 'You know that the rulers of the Gentiles lord it over them, and their high officials exercise authority over them. Not so with you. Instead, whoever wants to become great among you must be your servant, and whoever wants to be first must be your slave – just as the Son of Man did not come to be served, but to serve, and to give his life as a ransom for many.'

Before reading it a second time, remember that Jesus was following the hot and dusty road south along the Jordan towards Jericho and Jerusalem in the days before the Passover. He has tried twice already to explain to His disciples what lies ahead and they are confused and anxious. The party is quite a large one, as many pilgrims are coming down to Jerusalem for the festival, not just the disciples. Palm trees line the road; the sounds of the Jordan, of animals and pilgrims mix together. Fruit trees grow well here and some people are picking the fruit and eating it.

Quote – unquote

When God wants to perform in us and through us and with us some act of great charity, he first proposes it to us by his inspiration, then we favour it, and finally we consent to it.

Francis de Sales

Imagine yourself in the pilgrim party as you read the story for a third time, slowly and with your imagination fully engaged, and then keep silence for another 5 or 10 minutes, and try and hear and understand what Jesus is saying, and feel your own reactions to James and John and their mother. What is God saying about how he wants you to behave now? (Write down anything important in your journal.)

Drawing it together
Re-read Matthew 20.26-8 and say a simple prayer of dedication of the coming week. End by extinguishing the candle.

Thought for the week
Try out a number of imagination exercises using the stories which cluster around the birth of Jesus: The Annunciation; the Birth; the shepherds in the field; the arrival of the Magi. Countless artists and dramatists have re-envisioned these scenes over the centuries and you can have your own go at picturing them.

ACTION STATIONS

We've been exploring what is like to enter the presence of God, especially in the stories of Jesus. Are you remembering to take what you find there back into the story of your own life?

---

3 Your Kingdom Come, your Will be Done, on Earth as it is in Heaven

 Be Still

Settle down, light our candle, and start to call to mind the people with whom you share your life. Start with the closest, and slowly work outwards. Don't bombard God straight away with petitions for them: ask Him to bless them, and to show you what He wants most for them. Later you can join in His prayer, and in answering it too.

The Journey so far

How have the meditations gone? Not everyone has a great gift of imagination, so you may have been frustrated (and, anyway, we always want to move on more quickly than we are managing …). Stay with the journey: there are many ways to pray and something to suit every temperament. Then again, the scenes may have burst into life for you and brought a real encounter with Christ. If so, make sure you have kept a good record in your journal – drier times may come and you will be able to go back to these oases and drink at their wells.

Prayer Clinic: *Dryness*

Welcome to our third Prayer Clinic! I said last time that we would come back to feelings of dryness, desert, and the struggle to pray. There have certainly been long periods for me when prayer has felt very one-sided and empty – Alan Titchmarsh says a nun he knows calls it 'firing blanks'. So I feel I can speak with sympathy to fellow travellers in the wilderness, but that also means that I feel I am wearing a hat size too big when I suggest ways through. Nevertheless, every serious writer on prayer has travelled this way and the way-marks they have left can be signposts for us too.

Quote – unquote

Prayer is like watching for the Kingfisher. All you can do is
Be where it is likely to appear, and
Wait.

Ann Lewin, 'Disclosure' (extract)

Put simply, this sort of loneliness seems to usually be understood in terms of the way in which we, as parents, will stand back from our children, when they reach a certain age, to let them learn to walk without support, learn to cope for themselves with a crisis, make their own decisions, and so on. God wants us to grow into an adult relationship with Him, to be His grown-up children, so we can perhaps also imagine Him asking us to go through times of desolation as well as of consolation, so that we can learn more about ourselves and Him and, in particular, learn not to love Him just for the comfort He gives us but for who He is.

Like children, though, we tend to be more comfortable either leaving everything to God or manipulating Him to do what we want, and so we experience a struggle and well as the dryness. Perhaps you can also see now why I said before that struggle and dryness can be signs of moving on in prayer: we are coming out of the nursery and facing the challenges of growing up. But how can we keep moving on and not give in under the pressure?

I would like to suggest three things that might help.

First, in times like these we often run out of words, losing confidence in either our ability to pray the right thing or God's presence to respond. Set forms of daily prayer are a real blessing here – a skeleton to keep us in shape. The 'official' forms in the *Book of Common Prayer* or *Common Worship* and its offshoots are used by many people. Others look to Iona or the Northumbria Community, the Franciscans or other communities. A helpful addition is to start to compile a collection of favourite prayers written by others and use them in your own quiet times. To always follow our journey of prayer like this risks never building an individual relationship with God but, at this stage in the journey, it can be the helping hand of an older brother or sister and just what we need. If you have the gift of a prayer language, sometimes called the gift of tongues, that is also something that can help for the same reason. Even our groans to God can be a sort of prayer beyond words. As St Paul wrote, 'In the same way, the Spirit helps us in our weakness. We do not know what we ought to pray for, but the Spirit himself intercedes for us with groans that words cannot express. And he who searches our hearts knows the mind of the Spirit, because the Spirit intercedes for the saints in accordance with God's will.' (Romans 8.26-27)

Quote – unquote
A naval officer was once praying the Lord's Prayer with a friend in a remote corner of Iceland. 'Say it slowly', he said, 'each phrase weighs a ton.'
John Pritchard, 'How to Pray'

Secondly, your deliberate prayer times may be just the times when you feel the struggle and dryness most. Do not stop being committed to them – we have to face these things – but rather be ready to catch the other moments when the sun breaks though the clouds, whenever and wherever it is, and send up arrow prayers of thankfulness and love in those moments.

Thirdly, at times like this, our feelings and thoughts are likely to swirl around and be full of contradictions. We decide God does not exist, then tell Him so! We are angry with Him but long for Him. We blame ourselves and Him simultaneously. We believe everything and nothing. If you turn up some of the Psalms you should recognise the picture! You will find dozens of these songs of lament, so let them give you heart: you are not alone. Try reading them in your prayer times, perhaps even writing a psalm of your own. Do not be afraid to let all the feelings pour out, however powerful and contradictory they may feel. You will find it does you good.

Exercise

Read Psalm 22, noting how the feelings are very strong and swing between lament and praise. Remember that this was the Psalm that came to Jesus' lips on the Cross. Then have a go at writing your own individual psalm (in your journal), or turn a psalm into a song as I did with Ps. 139.

The beginning of Psalm 22

1 My God, my God, why have you forsaken me?
   Why are you so far from saving me,
   so far from the words of my groaning?
2 O my God, I cry out by day, but you do not answer,
   by night, and am not silent.
3 Yet you are enthroned as the Holy One;
   you are the praise of Israel.
4 In you our fathers put their trust;
   they trusted and you delivered them.
5 They cried to you and were saved;
   in you they trusted and were not disappointed.

A modern psalm

Oh Lord, thank You for rescuing me from myself,
For providing a ladder out of the abyss,
For sending the one I longed for, just in time,
For guiding me to a worthy and satisfying profession.
Thank You for giving me so much:
Home, husband, healthy child (please let the next be so too),
Family, friends and good fortune.
Please, God, don't take them away!
And why, God, when You have given me this much,
Do I, begrudgingly, give You so little?
There is so much to be thankful for:
For our beautiful world (which we spoil day by day),
For our wonderful bodies (which we abuse frequently),
For our consciousness of right and wrong (which we ignore),
For Art and Music and Literature (which we take for granted).
How dare we ask You not to let us suffer,
When You must suffer daily our ingratitude?
And yet I do.
Jilly Douglas

Psalm 139   *Tune: Picardy (French Carol)*

1 You have searched me Lord and you know me,
   You know when I sit and I stand.
   You perceive my thoughts as I form them,
   You know all my words as they're planned.
   You discern my daily goings out and in,
   You hold all my ways in your hand.

2   Where then can I hide from your Spirit?
    Where is there to flee from your face?
    Though I seek out heaven or the hell–pit
    You are there throughout time and space.
    Though I rise up on the wings of the dawn,
    Still your hand gives me tight embrace.

3   If I say the darkness will hide me
    And the light be night dark as may,
    Even darkness will not be dark then,
    And the night will shine as the day.
    For all darkness is as light to you,
    Lord who breathed life into my clay.

4   You have made my innermost being,
    In my mother's womb you wove me;
    Watched my unformed body framing,
    Wonderfully, fearfully me.
    All my days ordained were written in your book
    Before one of them came to be.

5   Search me then O God and know me,
    Test my anxious thoughts with your gaze.
    Forge me free from all that is evil,
    Faithfully to serve all my days.
    Lead me Father, Son and Holy Spirit, one,
    In your everlasting ways.

© David Thomson. Permission is given for non-commercial reproduction

 ## Teaching talk

'Your Kingdom come, your will be done, on earth as in Heaven'. This is the point in our prayer journey when we have to face the old enemy of our own wilfulness. Learning to submit ourselves to God, to have His will at the centre of our being, is a life-long task. I've tried to gather some simple tools to help with the daily challenge of that task. Each of them has the same aim: to get to grips

Big Issue

What do you want? You can have what you like ... Empowering everyone sounds great – but it turns living and loving, debating and disagreeing into a power game, in which the winner's truth takes all. But perhaps the real truth, however few battalions it has, has another sort of power after all, and where God's will is, there's a Way.

with small acts of obedience, which can encourage us in a challenge which might otherwise seem too huge to handle. Slightly artificially, I have made them into a five-finger exercise.The little finger is about self-emptying, willingly being the little one. In Philippians 2, we read that Jesus, 'who, being in very nature God, did not consider equality with God something to be grasped, but made himself nothing, taking the very nature of a servant, being made in human likeness. And being found in appearance as a man, he humbled himself and became obedient to death – even death on a cross!' (Philippians 2.6-8) In this exercise, call His example to mind and ask the Holy Spirit to show you what being little, being a servant, means specifically for you today. Listen carefully and obey immediately.

The ring finger has a strange property. If you hold your hand palm downwards and try to lift it on its own, it barely moves. It stands for the prayer of apparently weak surrender, which Jesus prayed in the garden of Gethsemane. 'Not my will but yours be done.' Jesus chooses not to go it alone but to go with God's plan. In this exercise, picture Jesus the servant. Ask him to highlight some part of your life where you are going your way, not God's. Decide to change and follow God.

A more traditional 5-finger prayer
Thumb: for those nearest to you.
Index finger: for those who point the way.
Middle finger: for those who lead.
Ring finger: for the weak.
Little finger: for yourself.

The middle finger is the tallest – so it has the greatest need to be humbled, like the victor in a Roman parade of triumph who was accompanied by a slave saying again and again, 'Remember, you are only human'. This finger represents the prayer of complete self-abandonment to God. Charles de Foucauld prayed it like this: 'Father, I abandon myself into your hands: do with me what you will. Whatever you may do, I thank you; I am ready for all, I accept all. Let only your will be done in me and in all your creatures.' In this exercise, repeat Charles de Foucauld's prayer slowly to yourself. Become conscious of one area where you are not happy to let God take control and perhaps change the arrangements. Ask yourself why you feel particularly threatened at that point. Ask God to help you trust Him to put even that into His hands, believing that He desires your true happiness even more than you do, and knows better than you how to achieve it. Ask Him to show you some little way of beginning to trust Him.

The index finger is so called because it points to things. It stands for the prayer of release, as we direct the things that burden us towards God. In this exercise, lift up towards God those whom you love; your hopes and plans; and also your enemies and grudges. As you direct them towards God, give them up into His hands and then try to close your hand and leave them with Him, to care for them and deal with them as He sees fit.

Finally, the thumb stands for thumbs up, for God's great 'yes' to the world in the Resurrection. In this exercise, let the landscape of your life open up to God: picture the light of his love breaking through the clouds and illuminating the dark patches in the landscape, a promise that, however dead they may seem, God has not forsaken them. Then, try to accept that God is better than you at Resurrection and leave them with Him.

Look at your hand for a moment while I recap. The little finger for the prayer of littleness and service; the ring finger for the prayer of surrender; the middle finger for the prayer of abandonment; the index finger for pointing things back to God; and the thumb for God's 'yes' in our life. It is worth remembering that this discipline of being obedient and little in the little things in life has been the nursery and hallmark of the saints far more than the achieving of great works and heroic actions. Perhaps one of these five-finger exercises could be the next step in prayer for you this week.

Exercise

Choose one of the 'five-finger' exercises and try it out.

Drawing it together

Say the psalm you wrote, or a Bible one, slowly. Extinguish the candle.

Story Box: In God's Garden

I found myself with time to pray the other week, and things on my mind. Jean had a cold that wasn't shifting. Deeper down, I was having one of those middle-aged moments when half of me was longing for a new challenge and the other half was voting for a quiet retirement as soon as possible! What *did* I really desire under God (always a good can-opener question in prayer) and what *was* His plan for me? Perhaps because we'd visited a stately home the day before, I started to imagine a grand garden and look for God in it. After poking around for a while and admiring the borders, I came across a young chap filling a watering can from a tap. (We'd met someone rather like him on our visit.) 'Hello! My Father is the Gardener. What do you want?' The killer question... As I struggled to answer, I could only really end up by saying, 'The Father's will.' 'Come and drink his water then.' And then I was led to an upper barn room, and he was offering me the bread and wine of communion. The sacrament of God's presence in the Now. And while in one sense my questions still remained, and probably always will remain (faith is not the same as fortune-telling), in a deeper sense I was restored to the Answer of God Himself. And oh yes, perhaps as some sort of sign, as I left the garden, the young chap showed me a plant for Jean's healing, I thanked God for her recovery, prayed for her, and the cold went.

 Thought for the week

Staying with obedience and prayer to place ourselves in God's will.

ACTION STATIONS

Keep a note of what you actually do differently as a result of your commitment to be doing God's will, and helping build His kingdom.

4 Give Us Today Our Daily Bread

Be Still
Settle down and light your candle, but this time put beside it your diary or calendar, and some of things that you will be (or have been) using during the day. Let the light shine onto and into them for a while.

The Journey so far
I hope you are being honest about the full range of your feelings and experience in prayer. Keep a record in your journal. If you have not plucked up the courage to talk things over with someone, then how about doing so this week? Being a solitary in prayer is the hardest of callings: nearly all of us need support and encouragement!

Prayer Clinic: *Self-centredness*
We are half way through the course and your prayer journey may be passing through some boggy country. The enthusiasm of beginning may have worn off and the excitement of practical outworkings lies ahead of us. It is boot camp time, learning the trade and accepting the discipline. As it happens, though, this puts you in just the right place to face and deal with another of prayer's enemies: what I call self-ness. It's a made up word and I mean it to include preoccupation with our own problems and so going round in circles; self-pity; and just plain old-fashioned selfishness.

> **Quote – unquote**
> Who sits in solitude and is quiet has escaped from three wars: hearing, speaking, seeing: yet against one thing shall he continually battle: that is, his own heart.
> *St Antony*

If you are stuck here, one of the signs will have been that the little five-finger exercises just left you annoyed or frustrated and feeling even more bogged down, instead of pointing you to small but helpful ways forward. So, what can help instead?

The first thing to say is that, this side of Heaven, we will always be stuck with our familiar selves and that, frustrated as we are by them, they are how God has made us. Are you trying to be someone else? Whose voice is it that you hear telling you that you have got to do better, be different? It is amazing how much energy we can put into disliking ourselves, feeling useless and all the rest. The fact that it is a trap not a truth is shown by the way in which just a tiny word of affirmation or bit of success, just a sunny morning or a quarter of an inch less waistline, can change everything – for a moment, until we start to condemn ourselves again.

Try asking yourself, instead, what is God's viewpoint on all this? Wouldn't He, like any loving parent, just want to stoop down and scoop us up into His arms and cuddle it all out of us? Since we probably fancy the same thing, maybe it's not such a bad idea to give some of our prayer time to just nestling up to God. Perhaps it is a lack of just that, of time to simply be with God without an agenda, that is part of the problem. So why not get under the duvet with God and a hot water bottle, cuddle up to the pillow, and tell the Almighty that it is His turn to do the praying? If you want to tell Him a few home truths, or have a cry, the pillow won't object – and neither will He. In Ignatius' Spiritual Exercises, the retreatant begins by spending a whole week asking for the spiritual grace of knowing him or her self to be loved by God, bathed in His love. Only then does the prayer move on to ask for the grace to be made like Christ, die to this world, and always choose God's way.

> **Quote – unquote**
>
> Enter into the inner chamber of your mind. Shut out all things save God and whatever may aid you in seeking God; and having barred the door of your chamber, seek him.
>
> *Anselm of Canterbury*

> **Quote – unquote**
>
> I have been driven many times to my knees by the overwhelming conviction that I had nowhere else to go.
>
> *Abraham Lincoln*

So, do not be afraid to go back to the beginning and seek God's love. Maybe you are like me and still have an inner core which is not completely healed, still vulnerable to feeling unloved and, like me, you need, from time to time, to have God's love ministered into it again. Sometimes, by the way, I find that I cannot do this without help: if you are the same, do ask for it!

Finally, just a word for those who feel the time is right to attack the self head on and go beyond the little steps of last week. Here are two ideas to consider.

First, you could try drawing up your own Rule of Life. You might be able to talk to someone in the Franciscan tradition about their rule of living as a starter: their Third Order members have to draw up a personal rule. If you decide to have a go, I suggest you involve someone else, as the rule is not worth making if we can keep it all the time, and not worth having if you always fall dismally short - so we need help to manage the boundary.

Or if that sounds too organised for you, how about going for a few basic maxims instead. You could look at St Thérèse of Lisieux's *Little Way*. In short, it was to seek out the manual job, to welcome unjust criticism, to befriend those who annoy us, and to help those who are ungrateful. My apologies: you will realise, I hope, that littleness does not mean easiness, if that is what you hoped for. As I said, any rule worth writing in the war against self is going to challenge us where it hurts. Perhaps the first step is to decide how serious we are and what help we need if we are going to make progress.

Let me finish with an anecdote to show that even a life of obedience has its funny side. St Thérèse shared her life with a particularly obnoxious sister nun and made it her business to befriend her as per her rule. When St Thérèse died, she had been so successful in her mission that the other sister boasted of how she, the obnoxious one, had always given the Saint so much pleasure by her company.

The Church in Wales Rule of Life

Loosely based on the Rule of St Benedict, this Rule is intended as a basic commitment for every Anglican Christian in Wales

In response to the love of God, Father, Son and Holy Spirit, I offer my life to God and commit myself to:

praying and listening to God daily, worshipping with the church and being fed by him in the Eucharist

growing in my understanding of God by daily Bible reading and reflection, and learning together with the church

serving God in my daily life and work

sharing God's gifts of time, talents and money with my neighbours, the church, the community and the world

Exercise

Basking Prayer! Get comfortable and then read Isaiah 43.1-7 and play some soothing music.

Isaiah 43.1-7

1 But now, this is what the LORD says –
he who created you, O Jacob,
he who formed you, O Israel:
'Fear not, for I have redeemed you;
I have summoned you by name; you are mine.

2 When you pass through the waters,
I will be with you;
and when you pass through the rivers,
they will not sweep over you.
When you walk through the fire,
you will not be burned;
the flames will not set you ablaze.

3 For I am the LORD, your God,
the Holy One of Israel, your Saviour;
I give Egypt for your ransom,
Cush and Seba in your stead.

4 Since you are precious and honoured in my sight,
and because I love you,
I will give men in exchange for you,
and people in exchange for your life.

5 Do not be afraid, for I am with you;
I will bring your children from the east
and gather you from the west.

6 I will say to the north, "Give them up!"
and to the south, "Do not hold them back."
Bring my sons from afar
and my daughters from the ends of the earth –

7 everyone who is called by my name,
whom I created for my glory,
whom I formed and made.'

Teaching talk

At this point, I have to confess that I have deliberately kept back the most obvious thing to do if you are stuck in a bog. That is, to shout for help! In a prayer bog, the best person to help us is God. However, many of us will have been taught that it is wrong to pray for ourselves. That simply is not true. We are on the next line of the Lord's Prayer, and it says, 'Give us this day our daily bread'. Hands up those who feel they know better than Jesus what we should do. In fact, He went on to tell His disciples to ask for everything they need: 'Ask and you shall receive, seek and you shall find, knock and the door shall be opened unto you'. Which of us, as parents, he says, would refuse to listen to our child in its need. In fact, we get great joy from meeting the need and not just when they are little. Often, it is their refusal to let us help which hurts. Surely it is the same with God. Do you remember how Abraham in Genesis 18-19 negotiates with God for the salvation of Sodom? If there are only 50 innocent people there, will you destroy it? 45? 40? 30? 20? 10? The Jewish tradition is full of this confident, yet respectful, prayer to God for very practical needs. Jesus Himself let the Syro-Pheonician woman talk him into healing her daughter, and taught His disciples to go on asking God for help, even if it was like disturbing a neighbour in the middle of the night for nothing more than a loaf of bread.

Quote – unquote

For spiritual blessings, let our prayers be importunate, perpetual and persevering; for temporal blessings, let them be general, short, conditional and modest.

Jeremy Taylor

Abraham scored 10/10 for confidence in prayer. What would you say your score was at the moment? If you are feeling adventurous, you could do this as a group, and work out the average. Hmmm.

I wonder how you did? The group exercise is not just pure silliness, in fact. Encouraging one another is an important aspect of all asking prayer. Jesus taught that, where two or three are gathered together in prayer, God will grant their requests, and in the experience of the church prayer groups have often proved very important. So far, the emphasis of this course has been on our own individual experience of prayer, but from now on I will be giving some attention to how we can pray together as well. This, too, is a classic antidote to self-ness in prayer, for obvious reasons.

Story Box: The Rocky Road

It was one of those times when I had been doing a particular job for a good while, and was getting rather tired – and a bit stale. Good friends in the parish bundled me off to a lovely place in the country where I could be stuck back together, and be helped to start listening to God again and not just the voices inside me.

I'm a hard case, though, and must have sometimes driven the folk there to despair with all my questions and rationalisations. (Despite the problems they bring, I still think they're worth it though: as one writer put it, you shouldn't have to check in your brain at the door to be a Christian.)

So I found myself going out for a long walk to try and get some perspective on it all. It was good agricultural land, and that for someone brought up in Sheffield before the Clean Air Act was a delight in itself. I started to see the work of farming and gardening as a sharing in God's work of creation, something at the heart of what it is to be human, not a strange rural diversion. That came in very useful when a little later I moved to a much more rural job …

But still the questions came, and the path was pretty rocky too, and perhaps I was getting lost? Then a hint of a whisper of a word of an answer, and more a ticking off than a 'Turn again Whittington': most roads in this life are rocky, stop whingeing – and when you get to a junction I'll give you a sign.

Rather later … He did.

Asking prayer has, of course, another dimension beyond petitions for ourselves, with which we are very familiar, and that is intercession or prayer for others, letting ourselves be a bridge or pleader between some other person or situation and God. Here again, prayer in a group can add an extra dimension to our intercession. The whole notion of one person praying for the need of a second person at the request of a third has deep resonance for me with our life as the Body of Christ.

But I wonder what your mental picture of a prayer group is? Head bowed, everyone praying aloud and earnestly in fluent English, with lots of 'just's and 'Lord's? Everyone, except you, that is, who are feeling terminally embarrassed and petrified as your turn comes. And yes, I too can remember a time when all I could manage was a half-remembered Collect. In fact, a good prayer group will have as much variety in it of silence and speech, praying with the mind and praying in the Spirit, standing and sitting, formal traditional prayer and free prayer, as there is variety in our individual ways of praying themselves. Why should any sort of prayer be excluded? That does, of course, mean that everyone in the group will have to cope with and support others who do not do things the same way as they do, but isn't that important for us a Christians anyway?

Exercise

Look at the prayer jigsaw printed below. Look at each piece and consider how it could profitably be used in a prayer group. See how the pieces fit together to make a cross. Now think about some big prayer needs in the world and then pray for the needs, using as many of the forms of prayer as you can: the needs need it!

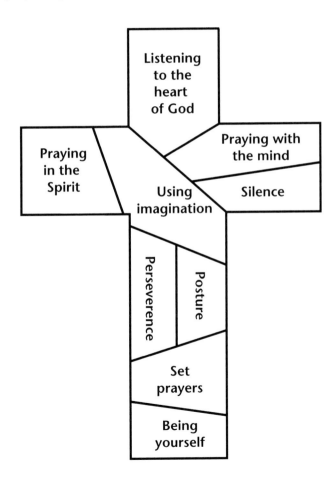

Drawing it together

Place your candle by the jigsaw cross. Ask God to be with you as you try to learn how to pray in new ways, and with the people and situations for which you prayed. Extinguish the candle.

Thought for the week

Go beyond the big, general needs of the world in your prayer and be a spy for God during the coming week, looking out in the local community for needs which you can take to God. Could you join or form a prayer group?

ACTION STATIONS

Here's a scary thought: keep a diary of all the things you consume during a week, and the things you do and surround yourself with to feed and comfort you. A mixed bag?

---

5 Forgive Us Our Sins, as We Forgive Those Who Sin Against Us

Be Still

If you have a moment, gather together a few pebbles or stones before you settle down and light your candle. Then put them round the candle as a sort of cairn – linking each stone with a person or situation that comes to mind that is 'hard' in some way. Then remember how long the stones have been around, how the elements in them trace back to the very dawn of creation, and how God was there then, and is here now.

The Journey so far

One of the problems some people find when they begin to take intercession seriously is that it can be simply overwhelming, either in quantity, or in weight. How has it been for you? Some folk find lists useful as a way of giving the prayer a manageable structure, though they are anathema to others! With a list it is possible to focus on today's items, pray for them, and then leave them with God until they next time they come round. I know several people who keep the Christmas cards they receive in a pile and pick one a day to look at and pray over (and perhaps send a letter or telephone afterwards), which is the same sort of idea. Unanswered prayer can also start to loom large as an issue, which is the subject of this week's clinic.

Prayer Clinic: *Unanswered Prayer*

Next please! Ah, yes, welcome back to the Prayer Clinic. We were thinking last week about prayers of asking, so today seems a good time to look at the problem of unanswered prayer. C S Lewis, and by now you will have realised that he is one of my favourite writers, once quipped, 'If God had

Quote – unquote

I have had prayers answered – most strangely so sometimes – but I think our heavenly Father's loving-kindness has been even more evident in what He has refused me.

Lewis Carroll

answered all the silly prayers I have made in my life, where should I be now?', and perhaps we have all prayed daft things like the famous 'Give me patience NOW' at some time or other. More seriously, we often pray for others with a very partial understanding of the situation, and what we see as good for them may well not be the best.

Having made the usual defences, I have to say that unanswered prayer is a real problem. You would think God would at least explain to us why He is not doing what we want but, so often, all we feel is a ghastly silence.

I keep going back to Jesus' own teaching on prayer and here we need to remember that His own prayer life passed through Gethsemane and Golgotha. Attempts to explain away 'My God, my God, why hast thou forsaken me?' as just referring to the triumphal conclusion of Psalm 22 fall short of even the exploration of that psalm which we made earlier; and equally unconvincing are bald statements that, from God's point of view, all prayers are answered 'as best for us may be'. We may, one day, find that that is true, but we cannot do so now.

We have to admit that prayer is an act of faith, not knowledge. Only in terms of faith does Mother Julian's 'all shall be well and all manner of things shall be well' make sense. It is the same act of faith that we make when we commend a loved one who has died into God's safe keeping, marry someone, or say in the baptism vows that, 'I believe and trust in God'. We can only decide to take the risk that God is indeed to be trusted, in the

---

Story Box: God is a Gambler!

That was the opening thesis of the sermon preached by a wise old Canon at his son's first celebration of the Eucharist as a priest. Assuming God knew his son as well as he did, the Canon went on, He was taking quite a risk in letting this young man loose on His church! The Canon was my father ...

---

sobering knowledge that if He is, He Himself has already taken the most monumental risk in trusting us with His world and our freedom.

So, when prayer is not being answered, what can we actually do?

First, it may well be true that we have not been as persistent as Jesus tells us to be and that we may be called to embrace the pain, not avoid it. Look at Elijah's actions in meeting the need of the widow of Zarephath in 1 Kings 17 for a rather extreme example of painfully committed prayer which bears fruit in the raising of her son.

The Widow of Zarephath's Son, 1 Kings 17

Some time later the son of the woman who owned the house became ill. He grew worse and worse, and finally stopped breathing. She said to Elijah, 'What do you have against me, man of God? Did you come to remind me of my sin and kill my son?'

'Give me your son,' Elijah replied. He took him from her arms, carried him to the upper room where he was staying, and laid him on his bed. Then he cried out to the Lord, 'O Lord my God, have you brought tragedy also upon this widow I am staying with, by causing her son to die?' Then he stretched himself out on the boy three times and cried to the Lord, 'O Lord my God, let this boy's life return to him!'

The Lord heard Elijah's cry, and the boy's life returned to him, and he lived. Elijah picked up the child and carried him down from the room into the house. He gave him to his mother and said, 'Look, your son is alive!'

Then the woman said to Elijah, 'Now I know that you are a man of God and that the word of the Lord from your mouth is the truth.'

Secondly, a simple equation between persistence and fruit is probably the exception rather than the rule, so it is important to be honest about what is going on. Keep a note in your journal about these long term prayer needs, so that your commitment and your frustration can both be expressed.

Thirdly, there may come a time when carrying this 'prayer burden' becomes just too much. At that point, you could try writing down the need on a piece of paper. It could be just a few words, or you could write it all out as a long letter to Jesus. Then, with a friend, take the paper and literally put it under the cross, perhaps in Church, perhaps at home. Pray that, as Jesus died for all the sins and frustrations of the world, so you might know that His death was also for the situation which is concerning you; that this too

Story Box: Iconostasis

We visited the little Orthodox shrine in Walsingham last summer. Some notes explained that an Orthodox church can be seen as a building of two halves. First the body of the church with all its comings and goings, icons and offerings, which is the space of our struggle on earth. Then the altar area which speaks of heaven, and of heaven and earth joined in worship in the Holy Eucharist. Between the two, of course, stands the iconostasis screen. Shut. As we sat and prayed I thought of how often the gate to God does seem shut, not open, despite all those nice prayer cards of open doors. Any approach to prayer that doesn't face up to the fact of its dryness and seeming one-sidedness at times is going to run into trouble sooner or later. The key, I think, to keeping going is remembering that we are Not Alone. On the one hand, God is as it were praying rather more for us than we are to Him, and has no intention of dropping us. And on the other, all those icons remind me that - past, present and future (which are not so different from God's point of view) - other people are praying with and for us too. A friend with terminal cancer shamed me recently with her joy that because friends and family were widespread it meant that someone somewhere was probably praying for her round the clock. Perhaps the closed door isn't as big a problem as it seems if such a cloud of witnesses and even God Himself are here on our side of it after all.

was a burden He took to the cross. According to the circumstances, you can then either take the paper back, with the trust that you are not carrying its burden alone and with the promise of God's help; or you can relinquish it to God's care and burn it as a sign that it is gone from your hands. Letting go like this can be the hardest thing in the world, but the thing you most need to do.

Exercise

Try out the letting go exercise. Write down a brief note of a concern that has been with you for some time. I suggest that it may be best, in this practice situation, to choose something that does not go too deep. Then put the paper under a cross, perhaps by the candle, and move into prayer, asking for the Holy Spirit to give you the gift of discernment to know whether you are called to carry on holding the prayer need or to relinquish it. You can leave your paper under the cross or burn it as a sign of letting go.

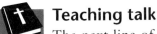

Teaching talk

The next line of the Lord's Prayer is distinctly challenging: 'Forgive us our sins, as we forgive those who sin against us'. I have to say that harboured resentments and unforgiveness are, in my experience, one of the most damaging things in an individual's spirituality and in the life of a church – and that I have found that the people in the parishes I have served have had their fair share of them. The inclusion of this line in the Lord's Prayer makes it clear that Jesus wants His disciples to deal with such problems and to use prayer as a tool in doing so. Strangely, you may also find that the releasing involved in giving and receiving forgiveness is what unblocks the jam of a long-unanswered prayer as well.

Receiving forgiveness for ourselves means, first, confessing that we have sinned. In the days when Holy Communion was celebrated less frequently, those who intended to receive it would prepare themselves by self-examination and, in some churches, formal confession. I don't know about you, but it is a long time since I did a full spiritual examination of myself – under, perhaps, the headings of the Ten Commandments. Meeting regularly a few times a year with a minister or friend, who has permission to ask all the awkward questions, is often recommended here.

It may not be right to get into very deep matters, unless you feel sure and have support. But I wonder whether you could use a little time now to do something privately about some of the smaller sins and bad habits that beset us all – like getting angry when we shouldn't, kicking the dog, not helping someone when we could have, and the like.

You could *either* write down a private note of some sin that you would like to know is confessed and forgiven and put in under the cross, then sign yourself with the cross, as a sign of forgiveness. Then destroy the note.

Or, alternatively, bring the sin to mind and mentally reach out with it to the Risen Christ and imagine Him looking at you with love and taking the sin away in His wounded hands.

'Because of our sins He was wounded, beaten because of the evil we did. We are healed by the punishment He suffered, made whole by the blows He received'. This glorious exchange, whereby Christ takes our sin and gives us His innocence, is at the heart of the Christian Good News. I hope and trust that, in the days to come, this active doing of what Jesus commanded us to do will open up a new dimension in your spiritual life.

Big Issue

For a tolerant, liberal society, we are surprisingly unforgiving. But in a humanistic world, or even the world of faith without Christ, who can legitimately wipe the slate clean of what we have done, with all its consequences? Many feel it outrageous that it should even be contemplated: a life for a life. But which of us is good enough then to merit a place in the sun? Redemption is vital – even if it does not compute.

However, we do also have to look at the other half of that Lord's Prayer line – forgiving others. If we do not do this, then Jesus makes it very clear that we will not feel the benefit of being forgiven ourselves. Again, a simple exercise can help. Call to mind some person that you need to forgive. Clench your hand and recognise that its grip is your unforgiveness holding on to the person you need to forgive, refusing to release them, and leaving you both unfree. It is not a matter of condoning their actions, or even of pretending that it never happened. It is all about not letting what did happen become the whole truth about that other person and ourself, condemning them to be seen by us in that light forever, not as John, but a liar; not as Jane but a gossip. We do not forgive the offence, but we need to forgive and release the offender.

After a while, open your hand and silently pray a prayer in which you tell God you have forgiven the person concerned. Then, stretch out your open hand in a gesture of release, towards the cross if there is one in the room. When you are ready, draw together all your forgiveness in a prayer of thanksgiving, release and protection. If the person you are thinking of now is someone you don't think you could release in this way, choose someone else for now, but talk the first situation over with a friend as soon as possible: God may be asking you to deal with it before too long.

Exercise

Try a prayer of release using the ideas above or any other approach that you are used to. In one of the Communion services of the Anglican church in Kenya, a prayer of release is part of the liturgy:

A Kenyan Blessing and prayer of release before the Cross

Leader: All our problems

All: We send to the cross of Christ (Sweep arm to the cross)

Leader: All our difficulties

All: We send to the cross of Christ (Sweep arm to the cross)

Leader: All the devil's works

All: We send to the cross of Christ (Sweep arm to the cross)

Leader: All our hopes

All: We set on the risen Christ (Sweep arm towards heaven)

Leader: Christ, the Sun of Righteousness shine upon you and scatter the darkness from before your path: and the blessing of God Almighty, Father, Son and Holy Spirit, be among you, and remain with you, always.

All: Amen.

Drawing it together

Make a short prayer of thanksgiving on this theme, concentrating on what God has done for us on the Cross. Extinguish the candle.

Thought for the week

Are there things that you need to forgive, or be forgiven for, as whole churches or communities? In Banbury, for instance, St Paul's Church was built for the poorer people because the carriage trade at St Mary's did not want to share a church with them. The same thing happened in Conisborough and in many other places. Some of the ways in which glebe land and old vicarages have been sold have left deep hurts in rural parishes. But, remember – if we look at these things it is in order to forgive the offenders and confess our own offences, not to dwell on old sores (or settle old scores!). Can you gather some people together and talk about it? How would you feel about confessing and offering forgiveness corporately? Is that valid? For some biblical examples, look, for instance, at Daniel 9 and Ezra 9, and at the promise in 2 Chronicles 7.14.

Corporate Confession: Ezra 9.5-6, Daniel 9.15-19, and 2 Chronicles 7.14

Then, at the evening sacrifice, I rose from my self-abasement, with my tunic and cloak torn, and fell on my knees with my hands spread out to the Lord my God and prayed: 'O my God, I am too ashamed and disgraced to lift up my face to you, my God, because our sins are higher than our heads and our guilt has reached to the heavens.'

... ...

'Now, O Lord our God, who brought your people out of Egypt with a mighty hand and who made for yourself a name that endures to this day, we have sinned, we have done wrong. O Lord, in keeping with all your righteous acts, turn away your anger and your wrath from Jerusalem, your city, your holy hill. Our sins and the iniquities of our fathers have made Jerusalem and your people an object of scorn to all those around us.

'Now, our God, hear the prayers and petitions of your servant. For your sake, O Lord, look with favour on your desolate sanctuary. Give ear, O God, and hear; open your eyes and see the desolation of the city that bears your Name. We do not make requests of you because we are righteous, but because of your great mercy. O Lord, listen! O Lord, forgive! O Lord, hear and act! For your sake, O my God, do not delay, because your city and your people bear your Name.'

... ...

If my people, who are called by my name, will humble themselves and pray and seek my face and turn from their wicked ways, then will I hear from heaven and will forgive their sin and will heal their land.

ACTION STATIONS

In case looking at things as a group distracts you – who precisely are you finding it hard to forgive at the moment (or had even forgotten that you needed to)? And what can you do about that?

6 Lead Us Not into Temptation, but Deliver Us From Evil

Be Still

As usual, light the candle in your prayer place. This time focus on the light itself. It is a powerful symbol – and more than a symbol. What we perceive as light is a basic building block of creation, the raw energy of the photon. In the simple chemistry of a candle the seemingly inert, even deathly, mass of the wax is transformed to release a power that speaks of life. Think for a moment of how God said and goes on saying, 'Let there be light.'

The Journey so far

Still stuck on forgiveness? What things came up in the church/community to ask forgiveness for, or forgive? What issues are hard for you personally? Try taking them to the light.

Prayer Clinic: *Temptation*

'Let us pray' sounds such a simple phrase but we do seem to have had some significant problems to deal with. Our progress through the Lord's Prayer brings us to another: temptation. If we take Jesus' temptation in the

Quote – unquote

Temptation reveals to us what we are.

Thomas à Kempis

wilderness as our model, then we immediately learn some important lessons.

First, it is the Spirit that sends Jesus into the wilderness, so, this testing must be something God allows. William Barclay wrote that, 'Temptation is not designed to make us sinners. It is designed to make us good'. By resisting it, of course!

Secondly, we note that Satan is the agent of temptation, permitted by God to act as such, as we see also in the Book of Job.

Thirdly, we learn that Jesus was not ashamed of His temptations – after all, only He could have told the Gospel writers about them!

When we make any attempt to grow spiritually, we will be tempted and tested. Perhaps you can call to mind what the temptations are that impact on your prayer life. For me, the need to feel warm and secure can be very strong, so, a threatening environment can throw me off course very quickly. I would probably have accepted the bread made from stones! Time and again I have had to learn to trust God for my physical needs. Half of me is very wary of power and glory, but the other half ... I do, however, have very little desire to throw myself from the church spire, just to create a sensation.

But what about you? The old seven deadly sins can give a quick health check: Pride, covetousness, lust, envy, gluttony, anger and sloth. Nasty bunch aren't they, but they don't half get around. In dealing with temptation, we may have to accept that the pull of sins like these is built in to our humanity, and work through our response to them in a matter of fact way. Telling our lust to go away as if it was something outside us can be a dangerous short cut. We do, however, need to renounce and repel the tempter, and the evil he wills us, with all our heart, and to be sure that we are properly 'in Christ', as St Paul puts it, and drawing on His strength.

The classic prayer way of doing this is to 'put on the whole armour of God', using the description of that armour in Ephesians 6.10-18:

> Finally, be strong in the Lord and in his mighty power. Put on the full armour of God so that you can take your stand against the devil's schemes. For our struggle is not against flesh and blood, but against the rulers, against the authorities, against the powers of this dark world and against the spiritual forces of evil in the heavenly realms. Therefore put on the full armour of God, so that when the day of evil comes, you may be able to stand your ground, and after you have done everything, to stand. Stand firm then, with the belt of truth buckled around your waist, with the breastplate of righteousness in place, and with your feet fitted with the readiness that comes from the gospel of peace. In addition to all this, take up the shield of faith, with which you can extinguish all the flaming arrows of the evil one. Take the helmet of salvation and the sword of the Spirit, which is the word of God. And pray in the Spirit on all occasions with all kinds of prayers and requests. With this in mind, be alert and always keep on praying for all the saints.

The idea is that we deliberately clothe ourselves with the habits, gifts and fruit of the Spirit and, so, simultaneously challenge ourselves to holiness and come under the strength and protection of God. We commit ourselves to living and telling the truth as God has shown it to us. We accept the righteousness that only Jesus can give. We take up His call to spread the Good News. We hold firm to the faith and God's Word in the Bible and let the great work of Christ, in winning our salvation, dwell in our mind. When we are dressed like that, there is little chance of the enemy taking advantage of our sinfulness, even when we give way to his temptations.

Big Issue

We seem schizophrenic about evil. On the one hand it is rationalised away, or seen as a sub-department of psychosis. On the other, we seem more ready to point to raw, unredeemable evil than to the simple, unquenchable goodness of God. A traditional Christian approach to evil is to see it as the absence of good and God; today we seem more comfortable reducing the good and God to a place-holder for the absence of evil. What is good is not news, and what is not news is not real …

Read the passage for yourself and try to make it yours in the way I have described. If it helps, you could make it part of your daily prayer, perhaps as you are dressing in the morning.

Exercise

Read out the passage from Ephesians slowly, pausing between the items of armour, taking time to reflect on them. Note how in every case we can think of them as an aspect of the nature or work of Christ that we are seeking to clothe ourselves with, not some sort of talisman.

Teaching talk

The armour passage from Ephesians talks not just about temptation but about a real battle between spiritual forces of good and evil. This may be something you find scary, or even hard to believe. My own view on this has changed over the years and experience has shown me that, difficult though it is to keep a right perspective, we cannot ignore this dimension of our faith. There it is in the Lord's Prayer: 'Deliver us from evil'; and Jesus Himself clearly saw His ministry in terms not just of encounters with people but with angels and demons too. As to what these words precisely mean – there is, I think, no right answer. Some will see them as impersonal, some as personal; some common, some rare. Anyway, the Bible does not encourage us to find out more about evil than we need to know to renounce it.

C S Lewis gets it about right for me again in his famous *Screwtape Letters*: 'There are two equal and opposite errors into which our race can fall about the devils. One is to disbelieve in their existence. The other is to believe, and to feel an excessive and unhealthy interest in them. They themselves are equally pleased with both errors and hail a materialist and a magician with the same delight.'

From the *Common Worship* Baptism Service

Do not be ashamed to confess the faith of Christ crucified.
Fight valiantly as a disciple of Christ
against sin, the world and the devil,
and remain faithful to Christ to the end of your life.
May almighty God deliver you from the powers of darkness,
restore in you the image of his glory,
and lead you in the light and obedience of Christ.
Amen.

Big Issue

Back in the '60s Jürgen Moltmann identified a lack of hope as a critical disease in Western society, and daringly drew on his experience of the concentration camps to proclaim the hope of the transformation of history in the coming of the Kingdom. Tom Wright more recently urges us to believe in God's breaking into our history, not our escape from it. What sort of real hope for our real world can we offer (with all its climate change and mutual assured destruction)?

Another help to me is that the familiar words of the baptism service can still speak with vigour and fighting valiantly under the banner of Christ against sin, the world and the devil; and that helps me along when other friends use language like prayer combat and spiritual warfare which is newer to my ears.

Language apart, should we join in on the side of the angels and, if so, how? At one stage in my ministry, I would have said that our main job is to concentrate on being good and let God take care of the devil. I think there is still some truth in that. But, if in human terms an evil empire like that of Hitler had to be resisted, I am now not so sure that a pacifist approach to spiritual evil is right after all.

Perhaps some of the confusions we see in the church and the world today are the result of the church withdrawing too much from confronting evil. So now I found myself considering how we, as the church, can 'stand up

Story Box: Blessing and Cursing

At one point in my ministry, when I had a good number of years under my belt and thought most of what could happen to a vicar had happened, I was brought up very short by a particular incident.

A parishioner decided to take exception to something that I had done: something I didn't myself see as wrong, though it was a complex enough situation to mean that I couldn't just go into self-defence mode and shrug it off.

The real problem was, I think, the very aggressive and threatening way the complaint was made. I started on a steep learning curve about coping with conflict (which has come in very useful now I am an archdeacon …).

What I found was that the feeling of threat was very hard to dislodge, and stayed around in my mind, poisoning the wells of my own spirituality and ministry, for week after week. Nothing seemed to make a difference – until eventually, on holiday during a cliff-top walk, it suddenly dawned on me to try what Christ said and bless the person who, in effect, by intention or not, had cursed me. I did – and in one of those rare moments, found an immediate and lasting release. Alleluia!

for Jesus' and 'fight the good fight', as the old hymns put it, without going over the top into witch-hunts and inquisitions.

Two key factors in what I will call sane spiritual warfare are: listening to God and listening to the world. We listen to God because, at the end of the day, it is His verdict that matters as to whether something is a good human activity, bad human activity, or evil at work. We need to pray for the gift of discernment between them. Sounding off our own ideas and calling things evil too easily can be very damaging.

We listen to the world because as Christians we try to keep away from sin and evil and so, hopefully, do not know too much about them! A few rumours; the odd personal experience. It is a very insufficient body of intelligence with which to go into battle. I said earlier that we should not seek to know too much about evil *per se*. What we do need to know about is the real personal situations of the people involved, the real pressures and the real personalities that are at work. Nothing goes down so badly as moralising from a distance: we have to get involved and ask God to sharpen our senses as to what is really going on.

With these two needs in mind, I want to suggest a rather different final exercise. It is called prayer-walking. After a short prayer for the Spirit to help you in both sorts of listening, go for a 10 minute stroll in the streets outside (physically, if you can; in your imagination, if you can't). Look as sharply as you can at the world around you, asking God to show you what needs require our intercession and what areas of life are the scenes of spiritual struggle. Then, come back and pray in whatever way seems helpful – remember the prayer jigsaw – for both the needs to be met and for God's victory in the areas of battle. Do remember that, for all the needs you see and struggles you perceive, it is God's world, and He was there long before you put your coat on!

So, finish with a verse of a favourite hymn and a good loud rendition of the Lord's Prayer, with a special emphasis on the last few lines, which we finally reach now:

'For the kingdom, the power and the glory are yours, now and for ever. Amen.'

 ## Exercise

Whether now or later in the week, try out some sort of prayer walk. If you feel embarrassed, you don't need to carry a placard saying what you are doing! I know people who have turned delivering Christian Aid envelopes and church magazines into prayer walks too.

Drawing it together

Extinguish the candle for the last time – but don't stop praying.

Thought for the week

Have a look back at your journal. Does any particular story seem to stand out from it. Where is your journey going next?

ACTION STATIONS

You might have to blow the candle out for the last time – but you don't have to blow out the candle of your life. What can you be about this week that will spread light in the darkness?

---

7 The Way Continues

Travel on, travel on, to the music that is playing,
The music that is playing night and day.
Travel on, travel on, to the music that is playing,
The music will be with you all the way.

In the kingdom of heaven is my end and my beginning,
And the road that I must follow night and day.
Travel on, travel on to the kingdom that is coming,
The kingdom will be with you all the way.

So ends one of Sydney Carter's powerful songs, so surprisingly sung in primary schools across the land. One of J R R Tolkien's songs (sung in this form by Bilbo as he leaves the Shire in *The Lord of the Rings*) is in my mind as well:

The Road goes ever on and on
Down from the door where it began.
Now far ahead the Road has gone,
And I must follow, if I can,
Pursuing it with eager feet,
Until it joins some larger way
Where many paths and errands meet.
And whither then? I cannot say.

Prayer is a journey that goes on. It will go on for us, and it goes on before and beyond us: it is something we make part of our life, and a life in which we come to take part.

Your praying will also, I hope, go on. At best it will not focus down for too long on books or courses about prayer, like this one, but become simply another way of being the person God is leading you to be.

All the same, some special and deliberate actions remain part of our praying. The emphasis of this book has been on the 'sitting and thinking' sort of prayer. So let me suggest that as a counter-balance you make some plans now for some 'getting up and going' prayer.

A few ideas to get you started:

Make a leisurely, walking-pace visit to one of the great pilgrim places of our country – or even abroad: Lindisfarne, Iona, Canterbury, Walsingham.

(At Walsingham, to slow you down, you are supposed to stop first at the Slipper Chapel, and walk the last mile or so barefoot or with a pea in your shoe!)

Take an Emmaus walk. Divide your time in two: set off and walk for the first half of the time, calling to mind the things that have been going on in your life, and have as it were a conversation with Christ about them. Then stop for a bite to eat and read the Scriptures (celebrate Communion if you are in company) and give thanks for the living presence of the Lord with you. Then it's back home to put it all into action!

Or try an 'awareness' walk. Remember how Jesus walked with His friends and would point things out, or make parables out of them. 'Consider the lilies of the field.' 'Do you see those great buildings?' 'A sower went out to sow.' Take a walk and ask God to open your eyes to what He might be saying to you through them. Don't be afraid to have a good pause on the way and just listen. You might bring back something from the walk to keep as a reminder of what you saw and heard.

Story Box: The Driftwood Cross

A year ago, I had the enormous privilege of a sabbatical – three months away from the normal routine to re-fill my tank, and catch up with old interests and old friends.

I spent part of the time visiting the northern shores, places where the saints of old had set sail and landed, prayed and preached – Lindisfarne, Iona, Whithorn, Man.

Pilgrimage, exile, and the 'green martyrdom' of life on the margins of society were part of their spirituality, and it was moving to look out to sea and think of Columba and Colman, Cuthbert and Kentigern, Aidan and Ninian adrift as it were for God.

I started to collect pieces of driftwood, and eventually made some of them into crosses, large and small, as a symbol of my own special time away from ordinary life with God, and my hope that back in the daily routine I would also be able to sense the currents of the Spirit, and sail with them.

As I finish this small book on prayer, my own prayer is that each of you who reads it will yourself know the supporting, guiding, grace of God as you journey on.

Feeding on Scriptures

- When it contains warnings, we heed them

- Where it contains promises, we claim them

- When it teaches us spiritual doctrines, we trust them

- When it contains clear commands, we obey them

Some Favourite Prayers

Almighty God, from whom all thoughts of truth and peace proceed. kindle we pray thee in the hearts of all men the true love of peace, and guide with thy pure and peaceable wisdom those who take counsel for the nations of the earth: that in tranquillity thy kingdom may go forward until the whole earth is filled with the knowledge of Thy love, through Jesus Christ our Lord.

1928 Prayer Book, For the Peace of the World

Almighty God,
unto whom all hearts be open,
all desires known,
and from whom no secrets are hid:
cleanse the thoughts of our hearts
by the inspiration of Thy Holy Spirit,
that we may perfectly love thee,
and worthily magnify Thy holy name;
through Christ our Lord.

BCP, The Collect for Purity

Almighty God,
you have made us for yourself,
and our hearts are restless
till they find their rest in you:
pour your love into our hearts and
draw us to yourself,
and so bring us at last to your
heavenly city
where we shall see you face to face;
through Jesus Christ your Son our Lord.

CW, Collect for Trinity 17, after St Augustine

Almighty God,
We thank you for the gift of your holy Word.
May it be a lantern to our feet,
a light upon our paths,
and a strength to our lives.
Take us and use us
to love and serve all people
in the power of the Holy Spirit,
and in the name of your Son,
Jesus Christ our Lord.

CW, Thanksgiving for the Word

Almighty God, Father of all mercies,
we thine unworthy servants do give thee most humble and hearty thanks for all thy goodness and loving–kindness to us, and to all men. We bless thee for our creation, preservation, and all the blessings of this life; but above all, for thine inestimable love in the redemption of the world by our Lord Jesus Christ; for the means of grace, and for the hope of glory. And, we beseech thee, give us that due sense of all thy mercies, that our hearts may be unfeignedly thankful, and that we shew forth thy praise, not only with our lips, but in our lives; by giving up ourselves to thy service, and by walking before thee in holiness and righteousness all our days; through Jesus Christ our Lord, to whom with thee and the Holy Ghost be all honour and glory, world without end.

BCP, General Thanksgiving

Be present, O merciful God, and protect us through the silent hours of this night, so that we, who are wearied by the work and the changes of this fleeting world may rest upon Thy eternal changelessness; through Jesus Christ our Lord.

Blessed Lord, who hast caused all Holy Scriptures to be written for our learning: grant that we may in such wise hear them, read, mark, learn and inwardly digest them, that by patience, and comfort of thy holy Word, we may embrace, and ever hold fast the blessed hope of everlasting life, which thou hast given us in our Saviour Jesus Christ.

BCP, Collect for the Second Sunday in Advent

Bring us, O Lord God, at our last awakening into the house and gate of heaven: to enter into that gate and dwell in that house, where there shall be no darkness nor dazzling but one equal light; no noise nor silence, but one equal music; no fears nor hopes but one equal possession; no ends nor beginnings but one equal eternity; in the habitation of Thy glory and dominion, world without end.

John Donne

Christ be with me,
Christ within me,
Christ behind me,
Christ before me,
Christ beside me,
Christ to win me,
Christ to comfort
and restore me.
Christ beneath me,
Christ above me,

Christ in quiet,
Christ in danger,
Christ in hearts of
all that love me,
Christ in mouth of
friend and stranger.

From St Patrick's Breastplate

Christ has no body now on earth but yours,
no hands but yours,
no feet but yours;
yours are the eyes through which he is to look
with compassion on the world;
yours are the feet with which he is to go about
doing good;
and yours the hands with which he is to bless us now.

St Teresa of Avila

Deep peace of the Running Wave to you.
Deep peace of the Flowing Air to you.
Deep peace of the Quiet Earth to you.
Deep peace of the Shining Stars to you.
Deep peace of the Son of Peace to you.

Celtic Benediction

Enable us O Lord God, to walk in thy way with integrity and cheerfulness, faithfully believing thy Word and faithfully doing thy commandments, faithfully worshipping thee and faithfully serving our neighbour; after thy pattern and in the Name of thy Son our Saviour, Jesus Christ.

Based on a phrase of Jeremy Taylor

Eternal God,
the light of the minds that know you,
the joy of the wills that serve you;

grant us so to know you
that we may truly love,
and so to love you
that we may fully serve you,
whom to serve is perfect freedom,
in Jesus Christ our Lord.

After St Augustine

Father of all, we give you thanks and praise, that when we were still far off you met us in your Son and brought us home. Dying and living, he declared your love, gave us grace, and opened the gate of glory. May we who share Christ's body live his risen life; we who drink his cup bring life to others; we whom the Spirit lights give light to the world. Keep us firm in the hope you have set before us, so we and all your children shall be free, and the whole earth live to praise your name; through Christ our Lord. Amen.

CW, Post–communion prayer

Give me my scallop-shell of quiet,
My staff of faith to walk upon;
My scrip of joy, immortal diet;
My bottle of salvation;
My gown of glory (hope's true gage);
And thus I'll take my pilgrimage.

Sir Walter Raleigh

Go forth into the world in peace;
Be of good courage:
Hold fast that which is good;
Render to no man evil for evil;
Strengthen the faint–hearted,
Support the weak;
Help the afflicted;
Honour all men:
Love and serve the Lord.
Rejoice in the Power of the Holy Spirit.

A Valediction

God be in my Head,
and in my Understanding.
God be in my Eyes,
and in my Looking.
God be in my Heart,
and in my Thinking.
God be in my Hands,
and in my Serving.
God be at my End,
and at my Departing.

From a Book of Hours 1514

God grant me the
SERENITY
to accept the things I cannot change,
COURAGE
to change the things I can, and
WISDOM
to know the difference.

Reinhold Neibuhr

God of love, whose compassion never fails;
we bring before you the griefs and
perils of peoples and nations;
the necessities of the homeless;
the helplessness of the aged and weak;
the sighings of prisoners; the pains of
the sick and injured;
the sorrow of the bereaved.
Comfort and relieve them, O merciful
Father, according to their needs;
for the sake of your Son, our Saviour
Jesus Christ. Amen.

After St Anselm

God, of thy goodness, give me thyself,
for thou art sufficient for me.
I may not ask for anything less
than what befits my full worship of thee.
If I were to ask anything less
I should always be in want
for in thee alone do I have all.

Julian of Norwich

Grant, Lord,
that we may hold to you without parting,
worship you without wearying,
serve you without failing;
faithfully seek you,
happily find you,
and forever possess you,
the only God,
blessed, now and for ever.

St Anselm of Canterbury

Grant, O God, that we may wait patiently, as servants, standing before their Lord, to know thy will; that we may welcome all truth, under whatever outward forms it may be uttered; that we may bless every good deed, by whomsoever it may be done; and that we may rise above all party strife to the contemplation of the eternal Truth and Goodness; through Jesus Christ our Lord.

Charles Kingsley

Grant, we beseech thee, Almighty God, that like as we do believe thy only–begotten Son our Lord Jesus Christ to have ascended into the heavens; so we may also in heart and mind thither ascend, and with him continually dwell, who liveth and reigneth with thee and the Holy Ghost, one God, world without end.

BCP, Collect for Ascension Day

Have you not heard his silent steps?
He comes, comes, ever comes. Every moment and every age, every day and every night, he comes, comes, ever comes. Many a song have I sung in many a mood of mind, but all their notes have always proclaimed, he comes, comes, ever comes. In the fragrant days of sunny April through the forest paths he comes, comes, ever comes. In the rainy gloom of July nights in the thundering chariot of clouds he comes, comes, ever comes. In sorrow after sorrow it is his steps that press upon my heart, and it is the golden touch of his feet that makes my joy to shine.

Rabindranath Tagore

I am no longer my own but Thine.
Put me to what Thou wilt,
Rank me with whom Thou wilt.
Put me to doing, put me to suffering.
Let me be employed for Thee or laid aside for Thee,
Exalted for Thee, or brought low for Thee.
Let me be full, let me be empty.
Let me have all things, let me have nothing.
I freely and heartily yield all things to Thy pleasure and disposal.
And now, O glorious and blessed God Father, Son and Holy Spirit,
Thou art mine and I am Thine.
So be it.
And the covenant that I have made on earth
Let it be ratified in heaven.

From the Methodist Covenant Service

I said to the man who stood at the gate of the year, 'Give me a light that I may tread safely into the unknown.'
And he replied – 'Go out into the darkness and put your hand into the hand of God. That shall be to you better than light and safer than a known way!'
So I went forth and finding the hand of God, trod gladly into the night. And he led me towards the hills and the breaking of the day in the lone East.

Minnie Louise Haskins, The Gate of the Year

Jesus, Master Carpenter of Nazareth, who on the cross, through wood and nails, didst work man's whole salvation; wield well thy tools in this thy workshop; that we who come to thy bench rough-hewn may by thy hands be fashioned to a truer beauty and a greater usefulness, for the honour of thy holy name.
Attrib. Eric Milner-White

Keep us, O Lord, while we tarry on this earth, in a serious seeking after thee, and in an affectionate walking with thee, every day of our lives; that when thou comest, we may be found not hiding our talent, nor serving the flesh, nor yet asleep with our lamp unfurnished, but waiting and longing for our Lord, our glorious King, for ever and ever.
Richard Baxter

Lighten our darkness,
Lighten our darkness, we beseech Thee, O Lord, and by Thy great mercy, defend us from all perils and dangers of this night, for the sake of Thy Son, Jesus Christ our Lord.
BCP, Third Collect at Evening Prayer

Lord, help us to live this day quietly, easily; to lean upon Thy great strength trustfully, peacefully; to wait for the unfolding of Thy will patiently, joyously; to face the future confidently, courageously.
St Francis of Assisi

Lord, I am not worthy that Thou should'st come under my roof, but speak the word only, and Thy servant shall be healed.
A Roman Centurion at Capernaum, Matthew 8.8

Lord, I believe: help Thou my unbelief.
The Father of a boy with an evil spirit, Mark 9.24

Lord, I shall be very busy this day. If I forget Thee, do not Thou forget me. Amen.
Sir Jacob Astley, before the battle of Edgehill

Lord, make me an instrument of your peace:
Where there is hatred, let me sow love:
Where there is injury, pardon:
Where there is doubt, faith:
Where there is darkness, light:
Where there is despair, hope,
And where there is sadness, joy.
Divine Master, grant that I may not so much seek
To be consoled as to console,
To be understood as to understand,
To be loved as to love.
For it is in giving that we receive,
It is in pardoning that we are pardoned,
And in dying that we are born to eternal life.
St Francis of Assisi

Lord, now lettest Thou Thy servant depart in peace;
For mine eyes have seen Thy salvation;
Which thou hast prepared,
Before the face of all people.
To be a light to lighten the Gentiles,
And to be the glory of Thy people Israel.
BCP, The Nunc Dimittis

May the power of your love, Lord Christ,
Fiery and sweet,
So absorb our hearts
As to withdraw them from all that is under heaven.

Grant that we may be ready
To die for love of your love
As you died for love of our love.

Franciscan Mid–day Office

My dearest Lord,
be thou a bright flame before me,
be thou a guiding star above me,
be thou a smooth path beneath me,
be thou a kindly shepherd behind me,
today and for evermore.

St Columba

Most merciful Lord,
your love compels us to come in.
Our hands were unclean,
our hearts were unprepared;
we were not fit
even to eat the crumbs from under
your table.
But you, Lord, are the God of our
salvation,
and share your bread with sinners.
So cleanse and feed us
with the precious body and blood of
your Son,
that he may live in us and we in him;
and that we, with the whole company
of Christ,
may sit and eat in your kingdom.

CW, alternative Prayer of Humble Access

Night is drawing nigh –
For all that has been – Thanks!
To all that shall be – Yes!

Dag Hammarskjøld

O God, from whom all holy desires,
all good counsels, and all just works do
proceed: Give unto thy servants that
peace which the world cannot give;
that both our hearts may be set to
obey thy commandments, and also

that we being defended from the fear
of our enemies may pass our time in
rest and quietness; through the merits
of Jesus Christ our Saviour.

BCP, Second Collect at Evening Prayer

**O God, who has prepared for them
that love Thee** such good things as
pass man's understanding: pour into
our hearts such love towards Thee, that
we, loving Thee above all things, may
obtain Thy promises, which exceed all
that we can desire. Through Jesus
Christ our Lord.

BCP, Collect for the Sixth Sunday after Trinity

O God, who hast bound us together
in this bundle of life, give us grace to
understand how our lives depend
upon the courage, the industry, the
honesty and the integrity of our
fellow men: that we may be mindful
of their needs and grateful for their
faithfulness, and faithful in our
responsibilities to them, through
Jesus Christ our Lord.

Reinhold Niebuhr

**O Lord,
support us all the day long**
of this troublous life,
until the shadows lengthen and the
evening comes,
and the busy world is hushed,
the fever of life is over,
and our work is done.
Then, Lord, in your mercy
grant us safe lodging, a holy rest,
and peace at the last,
through Jesus Christ our Lord.

after Cardinal John Henry Newman

O Lord, we beseech thee mercifully to receive the prayers of thy people which call upon thee; and grant that they may both perceive and know what things they ought to do, and also may have grace and power faithfully to fulfil the same; through Jesus Christ our Lord.

BCP, Collect for the first Sunday after Epiphany

O Lord, who hast taught us that all our doings without charity are nothing worth: send thy Holy Ghost, and pour into our hearts that most excellent gift of charity, the very bond of peace and of all virtues, without which whosoever liveth is counted dead before thee: grant this for thine only Son Jesus Christ's sake.

BCP, Collect for Quinquagesima

O Thou, who art the light of the minds that know Thee;
And the life of the souls that love Thee;
And the strength of the wills that serve Thee:
Help us so to know Thee that we may truly love Thee;
So to love Thee that we may fully serve Thee;
Whom to serve is perfect freedom.
Amen.

St Augustine

O Tree of Calvary
send your roots deep down
into my heart.
Gather together the soil of my heart,
the sands of my fickleness,
the stones of my stubbornness,
the mud of my desires.
Bind them all together,
O Tree of Calvary.
Interlace them with your strong roots,

entwine them with the network
of your love.

Chandran Devanesen

Preserve us, O Lord, while waking,
and guard us while sleeping,
that awake we may watch with Christ,
and asleep we may rest in peace.

Compline antiphon

Prevent us, O Lord, in all our doings with Thy most gracious favour, and further us with Thy continual help; that in all our works, begun, continued, and ended in Thee, we may glorify Thy Holy Name, and finally by Thy mercy obtain everlasting life, through Jesus Christ our Lord.

BCP, Collect at Communion

Since, Lord, Thou dost defend
Us with Thy Spirit,
We know we at the end
Shall life inherit.
Then fancies flee away!
I'll fear not what men say;
I'll labour night and day
To be a pilgrim.

after John Bunyan

Soul of Christ, sanctify me.
Body of Christ, save me.
Blood of Christ, refresh me.
Water from the side of Christ, wash me.
Passion of Christ, strengthen me.
O good Jesu, hear me,
Within thy wounds hide me,
Suffer me not to be separated from Thee,
From the evil enemy defend me,
In the hour of my death call me,
And bid me come to Thee,
That with Thy Saints I may praise Thee,
Through all Eternity. Amen.

The Anima Christi

Strengthen for service, O Lord,
the hands that have taken holy things.
May the ears that have heard your
word be deaf to clamour and dispute;
may the tongues that have sung your
praise be free from deceit;
may the eyes that have seen the tokens
of your love shine with the light of hope;
and may the bodies which have been
fed with your Body be replenished with
the fullness of your life.
South Indian Liturgy of Malabar

Teach us, good Lord, to serve thee as
thou deservest; to give and not to
count the cost; to fight and not to
heed the wounds; to toil and not to
seek for rest; to labour and to ask for
no reward save that of knowing that
we do thy will, through Jesus Christ our
Lord.
St Ignatius Loyola

Thanks be to Thee,
My Lord Jesus Christ,
For all the benefits
Which Thou hast won for me;
For all the pains and insults
Which Thou hast borne for me.
O Most Merciful Redeemer,
Friend and Brother;
May I know Thee more clearly,
Love Thee more dearly,
And follow Thee more nearly,
Day by day.
St Richard of Chichester

Thankyou, dear Jesus,
for all that you have given me,
for all that you have taken from me,
for all you have left me.
St Thomas More

The Lord bless you, and keep you:
The Lord make his face shine upon
you,
and be gracious unto you:
The Lord lift up his countenance upon
you,
and give you peace.
Aaron's blessing, Numbers 6.24–6

Thou hast given so much to us,
give one thing more, a grateful heart,
for Christ's sake.
George Herbert

Watch Thou, dear Lord, with those
who wake, or watch, or weep tonight,
and give Thine angels charge over
those who sleep. Tend the sick ones, O
Lord Christ. Rest Thy weary ones. Bless
Thy dying ones. Soothe Thy suffering
ones. Pity Thine afflicted ones. Shield
Thy joyous ones. And all for Thy love's
sake.
St Augustine

Some Books on Prayer

Modern Books

Wendy Becket, *Sister Wendy on Prayer* (Continuum, 2006)
Anthony Bloom, *School for Prayer* (DLT, 1970)
Mother Mary Clare, *Encountering the Depths* (DLT, 1981)
Alan Ecclestone, *A Staircase for Silence* (DLT, 1977)
Charles Elliott, *Praying the Kingdom* (DLT, 1985)
Richard Foster, *Prayer* (Hodder & Stoughton, 1992)
Joyce Huggett, *Listening to God* (Hodder & Stoughton, 1986); *Learning the Language of Prayer* (BRF, 1996)
Henri Nouwen, *The Return of the Prodigal Son* (DLT, 1994)
John Pritchard, *How to Pray: A Practical Handbook* (SPCK, 2002)
Michel Quoist, *Prayers of Life* (Gill & Macmillan, 1965)
Michael Ramsay, *Be Still and Know* (Collins Fount, 1982)
Margaret Silf, *Taste and See: Adventuring into Prayer* (DLT, 1999)
Rowan Williams and Wendy Becket (Compiled by Su Box), *Living the Lord's Prayer* (BBC, 2005; Lion 2007)

Older Classics

Jean-Pierre de Caussade, *The Sacrament of the Present Moment* (Collins Fount, 1981)
Julian of Norwich, *Revelations of Divine Love* (Penguin, 1966)
Brother Lawrence, *The Practice of the Presence of God* (Hodder & Stoughton, 1989)
Thomas à Kempis, *The Imitation of Christ* (Collins Fount, 1963)

Collections of Prayers

Angela Ashwin, *The Book of a Thousand Prayers* (Marshall Pickering, 1996)
Mary Batchelor, *The Lion Prayer Collection* (Lion, 1996)
Frank Colquoun, *God of Our Fathers* (Hodder & Stoughton, 1990)
Ruth Etchells, *Just as I am* (SPCK, 1994); *Safer than a Known Way* (SPCK, 2006); *A Rainbow-coloured Cross* (SPCK, 2007)
Colin Podmore, *Prayers to Remember* (DLT, 2001)

Daily Prayers

Society of St Francis, *Celebrating Common Prayer* (Mowbrays, 1994)
The Northumbria Community, *Celtic Daily Prayer* (Marshall Pickering, 1994)
Time to Pray (Common Worship) (Church House Publishing, 2006)
David Adam, *The Rhythm of Life: Celtic Daily Prayer* (SPCK, 2006)

Also by David Thomson

Journey with John (Authentic, 2004, ISBN 978-1-85078-561-3)
Lent with Luke (Authentic, 2005, ISBN 978-1-85078-597-2)
Christmas by Candlelight (Authentic, 2006, ISBN 978-1-85078-699-3)

References

Church of England Prayer Books

BCP = Extracts from The Book of Common Prayer, the rights in which are vested in the Crown, reproduced by permission of the Crown's Patentee, Cambridge University Press

CW = Common Worship © Archbishop's Council of the Church of England 2000

1928 Prayer Book = The 1928 Book of Common Prayer (OUP, 1993) © Archbishop's Council of the Church of England 2000

Other references

4 C S Lewis, *Mere Christianity* (Geoffrey Bles, 1952), 156

5 Joyce Huggett, *Learning the Language of Prayer* (BRF, 1996), 13
   C S Lewis, *Screwtape Letters* (Geoffrey Bles, 1942), 25
   C S Lewis, *Letters to Malcolm: Chiefly on Prayer* (Geoffrey Bles, 1964), 19

6 Rowan Williams and Wendy Becket (Compiled by Su Box), *Living the Lord's Prayer* (BBC, 2005; Lion 2007), 24-7

13 Julian of Norwich, *Revelations of Divine Love*, ch. 41(Penguin, 1966), 125

14 Sr Wendy Becket, *Sister Wendy on Prayer* (Continuum, 2006), 29

15 Rowan Williams and Wendy Becket (Compiled by Su Box), *Living the Lord's Prayer* (BBC, 2005; Lion 2007), 31

16 Photo David Thomson; included by kind permission of the Dean and Chapter, Ely Cathedral

19 Ann Lewin, *Watching for the Kingfisher*, 'Disclosure' (Foundery Press, 2004)

20 Alan Titchmarsh, *Trowel and Error* (Hodder & Stoughton, 2002), 43-4

21 John Pritchard, *How to Pray: A Practical Handbook* (SPCK, 2002), 17

22 Jilly Douglas' psalm was written during the Cockermouth course

29 See e.g. T N Taylor (ed.), *The Story of a Soul (L'Histoire D'une Ame): The Autobiography of St. Therese of Lisieux* (Echo Press, 2006)

29 See e.g. http://www.churchinwales.org.uk/monmouth/serving/rule/

39 Rowan Williams and Wendy Becket (Compiled by Su Box), *Living the Lord's Prayer* (BBC, 2005; Lion 2007), 61

41 Anglican Church of Kenya, *Our Modern Services* (Uzima, 2002), 84

46 *Common Worship: Services and Prayers for the Church of England: Christian Initiation* (CHP, 2005), 68

49 Sydney Carter, 'Travel On' in G Marshall-Taylor (comp.), *Come and Praise* (BBC, 1978), 65

49 J R R Tolkien, *The Lord of the Rings: Fellowship of the Ring* Vol 1 ch. 1 (HarperCollins, 2001)

54 The Covenant Service is printed in *The Methodist Worship Book* (Methodist Publishing House, 1999), 108-12

56 The Franciscan Mid-day Office (for Friday) is in Society of St Francis, *Celebrating Common Prayer* (Mowbrays, 1994), 14